STO   FRIENDS   2/01
       OF ACPL

THEY DIED TOO YOUNG

JOHN BELUSHI

Mary Hughes

CHELSEA HOUSE PUBLISHERS
Philadelphia

© 2001 by Chelsea House Publishers, a subsidiary of Haights Cross Communications.

The Chelsea House World Wide Web address is http://www.chelseahouse.com

Printed and bound in The Hashemite Kingdom of Jordan.
First Printing
1 3 5 7 9 8 6 4 2

Cover photo: John Belushi (Universal Pictures)

Library of Congress Cataloging-in-Publication Data
Hughes, Mary.
   John Belushi / Mary Hughes.
      p. cm. — (They died too young.)
   Including bibliographical references and index.
   ISBN 0-7910-5853-0
   1. Belushi, John. 2. Comedians—United States—Biography—Juvenile literature. [1. Belushi, John. 2. Comedians. 3. Actors and actresses.] I. Title. II. Series.
PN2287.B43 H84 2000
792.7'028'092—dc21
[B]
                                                          00-038385
                                                              CIP

Picture Credits: Columbia Pictures: p. 42; Corbis: pp. 8, 14, 16; Straight Arrow Publishers: p. 40; Universal Pictures: pp. 4, 22, 26, 30, 32, 35, 37, 38, 41

Publishing Coordinator Jim McAvoy
Editorial Assistant Rob Quinn
Contributing Editor Amy Handy

ABOUT THE AUTHOR

Mary Hughes graduated from the University of Maryland with a degree in Radio, Television, and Film. She enjoyed substitute teaching for many years before tackling her current assignment as a computer lab tech at an elementary school in Maryland.

   Her first book, a biography of comedian Jim Carrey, written for Chelsea House's OVERCOMING ADVERSITY series, was named to the New York Public Library's list of "Best Books for the Teen Age," 1999.

   An avid baseball fan, Ms. Hughes writes feature articles about ballplayers in the Baltimore Orioles organization. Writing as she does about both the minor and major leaguers, she often gets an inside peek at just what it takes to make it to the big leagues, and how special it can be to remain there. Her favorite ballplayer is her teenage son, Mark Hudson.

CONTENTS

The Pinnacle of Success	5
Cutting the Apron Strings	9
Saturday Nights Live	17
Making Movies	23
Brother Blue	33
Dividing a Continent	39
Farewell to a Friend	43
Further Reading	47
Chronology	47
Filmography	47
Index	48

John Belushi in *Continental Divide*.

THE PINNACLE OF SUCCESS

A good film begins with a good script, and the one written by Lawrence Kasdan was a gem. As soon as movie producer Steven Spielberg read *Continental Divide,* he recognized both the talent of the writer and the merit of the script and set about bringing it to the screen. Spielberg envisioned *Continental Divide* as a sort of modern-day verbal sparring match between its two costars, much like the delightful classic films that had starred Spencer Tracy and Katharine Hepburn.

Spielberg even had a hunch as to who should play the leading man—comedian John Belushi. He had loved this actor's character in the movie *Animal House.* And he had worked with John as fighter pilot Wild Bill Kelso in one of his own productions, *1941.* So, when the names of such box-office biggies as Richard Dreyfuss, Dustin Hoffman, and even Robert Redford were bandied about in Hollywood's casting circles, Spielberg took action. He knew he wanted John to play the muckraking Chicago newspaperman Ernie Souchak in *Continental Divide.* In fact, Spielberg personally handed John a copy of the script to consider.

Interviewed for Bob Woodward's biography *Wired: The Short Life and Fast Times of John Belushi,* Spielberg remembered the emotional roller coaster of a phone call he received after John had read the script. John was clearly wrestling with the idea of playing the role that was loosely modeled on his family's longtime friend, Chicago newspaper columnist Mike Royko. Spielberg recalled Belushi's words running the gamut from "I can't play him," to "I want to play him, I need to play him," to "I'm afraid, I hate it, I can't."

For John Belushi, the offer was almost too good to be true. Having spent nearly his entire acting career working in ensemble casts (meaning there was no main character), he was being offered a true leading man role. Granted, the film would have its share of supporting cast members, but he and the female lead would largely carry the film if it succeeded. And if it failed, John and his leading lady would be the ones held accountable.

For the first time in a long while, John wouldn't be surrounded by the actors he had worked with through most of his career. From *Saturday Night Live* to the films *Animal House, 1941,* and *The Blues Brothers,* he had worked with actors from the Second City Comedy Troupe.

This group of actors worked mostly on an improvisational basis—only loosely following a script while making up the rest. In this film he'd be engaging in small talk. There'd be clever conversations designed to delineate a boy-meets-girl relationship as it changes from one of hate to deepening attraction and love. There would even be love scenes!

How could he even think about playing a love scene? He was a good 40 pounds overweight. But he could hire a personal trainer, and with proper diet and exercise he could lose the 40 pounds. And love was not a foreign entity to John Belushi.

So the character Ernie Souchak was miserable when he was away from his love interest, Nell Porter. John felt fine with that, knowing all about the lovesick loneliness a man feels when he's away from the one he loves. He loved his wife, Judy, with all his heart and missed her terribly whenever she couldn't accompany him on location.

He felt comfortable getting the role because Mike Royko was practically family. John's uncle Pete Belushi was godfather to Mike Royko's oldest child.

By the time a meeting was arranged at Steven Spielberg's house, John Belushi was no longer considering whether or not he wanted to accept the role of Ernie Souchak. According to Spielberg's account, John began drinking and pleaded with those present to let him have the part.

John's overly animated "audition" that night nearly backfired, scaring off the duo that Spielberg had chosen for the project, director Matthew Robbins and producer Hal Barwood. Belushi's boisterous behavior and his drinking frightened Robbins and Barwood into looking for a different leading man, and eventually the two abandoned the project entirely.

Spielberg also had doubts about directing John after he'd seen that side of the actor. In the end, Spielberg relinquished his own directing rights to the film, settling for $100,000 and the title of executive producer. Universal Pictures brought in Michael Apted to direct *Continental Divide*, starring John Belushi as Ernie Souchak.

John, meanwhile, set off on a grueling concert tour with the Blues Brothers. When that ended, he and Judy went to Europe for a much-deserved vacation. Upon their return to the States, John knuckled down with personal trainer Bill Wallace, determined to get in shape with one month to go before *Continental Divide* would begin filming in October 1980.

In preparation for filming, Judy Belushi rented a large house in Canon City so the couple could be close to the film's initial location in the mountains of Colorado. The home was roomy enough to provide lodging for John's trainer. Also staying with them would be Smokey Wendell, whom John had once again hired to make sure that he steered clear of the drugs that Belushi believed were inevitably present in the company of the rich and famous. John recognized his own weakness to resist the drugs so often readily available.

Belushi's usual cast of characters were not to be found in Colorado that October. Instead, John had with him an entourage of a smaller, different sort. He had deliberately surrounded himself with people who had his best interests at heart. His personal trainer, Wallace, would help him stick to his healthful new diet and exercise regime. His personal truant officer, Wendell, would help him remain drug-free. And Judy would help the Colorado location seem less lonely and more like home. Tipping the scales at 199, having successfully shed 40 pounds, Belushi was ready to make his debut as a leading man in a major motion picture.

John with Sissy Spacek and Gilda Radner in a skit from *Saturday Night Live*.

CUTTING THE APRON STRINGS

John Adam Belushi was born on January 24, 1949. His father, who had emigrated from Albania, was very proud that his son John was the first Belushi boy to be born in America. Two years younger than his sister, Marian, John was the first of three boys born to Agnes and Adam Belushi. Jimmy and Billy followed.

Adam worked hard as a short-order cook at a Chicago restaurant. Several blocks away, Adam's brother Pete was also slaving over a hot stove, grilling cheeseburgers. The burger-flipping brothers had no way of knowing that their popular Chicago eateries would wind up being spoofed on late-night television once John joined the cast of *Saturday Night Live*. They were only manning the grills so that one day they'd be able to open a nice family restaurant. Eventually, the brothers Belushi realized their dream, serving up prime rib in Chicago's Morton Grove, at their restaurant, Fair Oaks.

But that dream was the dream of Albanian immigrants, not that of American-born John Belushi. He did work for a time as a busboy in his father's restaurant, but he repeatedly turned down his dad's offers to take over the family business.

Although Adam and Agnes Belushi didn't quite understand their son's interests in music and sports, they did their best to be supportive of all their children and were proud of them. Early on, John Belushi's dream was to become a professional drummer in a marching band. So when John asked his folks for a drum set, they took out a loan and got him one. Although John would later abandon his dream of drumming professionally, he would never give up his passion for music.

John's next dream was to play or coach professional football. Young John was a natural athlete. At the age of six his family moved from the city of Chicago to the suburb of Wheaton in northeastern Illinois. He was cocaptain of Wheaton Central High School's football team. "Killer Belushi," as his teammates called him, was 5 feet, 9 inches tall and weighed 170 pounds. Serious about his sport, Belushi was named to the All-Conference Team as a middle linebacker.

He was popular with his fellow classmates and was awarded the title "Most Humorous." He was also crowned homecoming king at Wheaton's annual homecoming dance in 1966. His date for the evening was Judith Jacklin. In her book, *Samurai Widow,* she recalled that John was a little embarrassed by the crowning ceremony. He was much more comfortable on the football field than he was posing for pictures with the homecoming queen, wearing a crown that was too small for his head.

Judy and John had not been dating long when they attended the homecoming dance together. They had only met late that summer at the local Little League field, each of them hanging out with their respective friends. Days later, again out with friends, the two met up for a second time, this time at Herrick Lake. Typical teenagers, the group began horsing around on the lake in the two boats they had rented. In the playful water fight that ensued, John inadvertently caught Judy's arm with the backswing of his oar.

That little mishap set a chain of events into motion. John was instantly apologetic. Judy recalled, "He immediately dropped the oar and began gently rubbing my arm, his face showing concern, almost anguish, that he might have hurt me. He apologized repeatedly. That night he phoned and asked how my arm was. I said it was fine and we talked briefly. The next night he called again with the same question, and I laughed. We talked for some time. Calling and asking about my arm became a running joke for about a week. Finally, John changed his question and asked if I'd like to go to the Homecoming Dance. I said I would."

From that boating excursion on, Judy and John's lives

were to be forever intertwined. Six months into their relationship they broke up briefly, largely because John didn't approve of Judy drinking with her friends. They were all underaged, and to make matters worse, were mixing driving with drinking. Two of Judy's friends would die before turning 18 as the result of two alcohol-induced car accidents.

Older than Judy, John was protective of her. She would soon come to realize that his caring stemmed from his love for her. It didn't take her long to realize that she was happiest when she and John were together, and that she was miserable without him.

Judy professed her love to John in a note. John let Judy know what their friends had already figured out: he loved her too.

Before he graduated from Wheaton Central in 1967, a teacher there would influence John in a way that would affect the rest of his life. His dreams of football began to fade once he discovered the lively art of theater.

In drama teacher Dan Payne's class, John found that he enjoyed acting. He had once ripped a T-shirt to shreds by the time he was finished impersonating Marlon Brando, and he had also turned in a solid performance in one of Wheaton's variety shows. John's acting impressed his teacher enough for Payne to wrangle an audition for John at a summer stock theater in Bloomfield, Indiana. Payne even drove Belushi to the audition himself, helping to soothe John's jitters en route.

More than 50 people, most of them college students or graduates, were vying for a chance to win one of the 12 jobs at Shawnee's Theater that season. The acting jobs didn't pay much: $45 a week. John's father had already told John that he'd have to bring in at least $50 a week that summer. Dan Payne knew what Adam Belushi expected John to earn each week. He also knew what Adrian Rehner's summer theater paid its resident actors.

So, when Rehner took Payne aside to let the drama teacher know how well he thought John's audition had gone,

Payne made a deal with the director. Payne wanted the theater to pay Belushi $50 a week, so that John's father would be satisfied. Payne would personally reimburse the theater for what amounted to an extra $5 a week, for the seven weeks of work. Rehner agreed. He didn't want to miss the chance to have John Belushi join his Shawnee acting troupe.

It didn't matter to Rehner that Belushi was coming to him fresh out of high school or that Belushi would become the youngest paid actor ever to be hired by Shawnee Theater. The kid had made everyone at the auditions laugh. Belushi had more talent than anyone Rehner had ever seen.

John Belushi didn't know about the $35 "bonus" that Dan Payne had personally allocated for his summer paychecks. He only knew that he was offered a job as a resident actor.

Bitten by the acting bug, John turned down a football scholarship from Western Illinois University, hoping he'd get into Illinois Wesleyan instead. He didn't. John made alternative plans to attend the University of Wisconsin at Whitewater in the fall, before he headed off to Indiana for seven weeks of theater.

John Belushi missed his high school sweetheart when he was away pursuing his acting career that summer and lovingly sent Judy letters detailing each production. He shared his triumphs and admitted his failings, all the while reminding her of his love.

The letters painted a picture of a young man coming of age, away from home for the first time in his life. His motorcycle, an inexpensive alternative to a costly car, provided him with transportation, even if he was constantly having to repair it, drawing stares from the people of Bloomfield whenever he rode through town. Adam had given the bike to John in 1965.

The late-night schedule John adopted that summer, which revolved around his theatrical performances, was one that suited him quite well. He liked staying up late, talking with friends, listening to the new *Sgt. Pepper*

Beatles album or even just riding his BMW 250 bike alone.

The drinking that the others seemed to enjoy didn't appeal to Belushi. He was trying to lose weight, so he didn't want the extra calories. That would just defeat the purpose of his workouts. And he didn't like the way getting drunk made people get sick or feel hungover the next day. Instead, he tried the marijuana he was offered. In a letter from July 1967, he confessed to Judy that he had smoked pot.

During those days at the Shawnee Summer Theater, John became the consummate "team player," building sets (which required good carpentry skills) and taking on all sorts of roles, even when it meant he had to shave off his beard, as he had to for his role in *John Loves Mary*. It was in *The Tender Trap* that John Belushi first took on the role of a jazz musician, wearing dark sunglasses to look the part.

Payne was pleased to hear how well Belushi had fared with his summer stock acting. Before the summer was over, Dan and his wife, Juanita, treated John to another peek at performing. They took him and Judy to see Chicago's Second City Comedy Troupe. Before the evening of sketches and improvisation was over, John was convinced that he could do what the actors and actresses were doing onstage. And he wanted to join them.

With a summer of theater under his belt, John headed off to college at the University of Wisconsin in the fall. Still self-conscious about his weight, he joined the school's karate club to keep up with his exercising.

John was proud to be one of only three boys cast in a college production and the only freshman. He was also happy that his director had told him he wouldn't have to shave off his beard, which he had just grown back.

Because John was attending college during such a tumultuous time, there was a lot going on around him. Students were rioting and protesting. Belushi did his best to stay informed about the issues of any given protest, which often revolved around civil rights. He was only in favor of those

John with Bill Murray on *Saturday Night Live.*

protests he believed were in the best interest of the school, its students, and the country.

Judy, who at the time was still attending Wheaton Central High and was very active in the school's student government, wrote to John, suggesting he join a fraternity. Belushi fans who would later love his Bluto character in the movie *Animal House* might have been surprised at the response John wrote to Judy. He spelled out most emphatically that he did not want to be "a frat rat who only thought about the next beer party," who thought that "all that 'brotherhood' crap and being childish were more important than their own country."

John's days at the university were numbered. His father simply couldn't afford to send him there for a second year.

They Died Too Young

After finishing his freshman year, John returned to the Wheaton area, renting a barn there with two of his friends. He worked odd jobs that summer to come up with his part of the $40 monthly rent.

That fall he transferred to the College of DuPage in Glen Ellyn, Illinois, a community college closer to home and to Judith. To keep his hand in theater, John started up a comedy group called the West Compass Players with his friends Tino Insana and Steve Beshekas. Under John's direction they performed skits in the student union on campus, and at coffeehouses off campus.

In the fall of 1969, Judy went off to college at the University of Illinois at Urbana-Champaign. John remained in Wheaton, finishing up his DuPage course work. Not long after Judy left for school, Dan Payne had a heart-to-heart talk with John. He knew that John had once wanted to coach football. In a September letter to Judy after that conversation, John wrote that Dan felt "responsible for getting me involved with theater and thought I might want to have a secure job, like coaching." But by then John had long since made up his mind. He had returned from his season of summer stock theater at Shawnee determined that he was going to be an actor.

John Belushi graduated in 1970 with an associates of the arts degree in general studies from the College of DuPage. To celebrate, he hitchhiked across America.

John doing his legendary impersonation of rocker Joe Cocker.

SATURDAY NIGHTS LIVE

In 1971, John realized a dream by joining Chicago's Second City Comedy Troupe. His audition had impressed one of Second City's founders, Bernard Sahlins, who had seen talented performers before. He had auditioned and cast comedians Robert Klein, David Steinberg, and Joan Rivers.

Just as John had been the youngest performer hired at Shawnee Summer Theater, he was the youngest performer ever to join Second City. At 22, he quickly became its star performer. He played a variety of parts, relying on his impersonation and improvisational abilities. Working through the rehearsed skits as well as the improvised sketches, he tackled everything from Hamlet to hippies. His impressions of author Truman Capote and Chicago Mayor Richard J. Daly soon became audience favorites. He concocted a character comprised of one part Elton John, one part James Taylor, and dubbed him Elton Taylor. Then, delving deeper into the world of music, John came up with a gem of an impersonation that virtually guaranteed hysterics every time he brought it to the stage.

Singer Joe Cocker's voice was so raspy and his body movements so erratic onstage that he was practically a parody of himself. Once audiences realized that Cocker would indeed survive his songs to sing again, they breathed a collective sigh of relief. Then suddenly, as is often the case in such situations, it was okay to make fun of his bizarre stage presence.

Enter John Belushi. Because Belushi's fans immediately realized that what John was doing onstage was just an act, they were not in the least bit afraid to laugh. Right from the start, they were comfortable laughing at Belushi's manic motions. But as John took the impersonation to ridiculous levels, maximizing everything for comic effect, even falling to the floor to exhibit his total absorption into the character, it was the audience that began to convulse—with uncontrollable laughter.

Just as the summer at Shawnee had lent itself to a late-night lifestyle, so did John's all-consuming job with Second City. The workweek was spent largely with other cast members, everyone gearing up for the shows at week's end. Then there was an almost imperceptible lull before the chain of events swung back into motion for the following week's shows.

Mondays were the only days off. Every other day, John and the other members of the troupe were expected to be "on." Getting "high" was one way that some performers dealt with their demanding schedules. Belushi was no exception. He now smoked marijuana on a regular basis. He tried other drugs as well, experimenting with new ones as they came on the scene.

John's famous impression of Cocker gave him a big break. The touring comedy show *National Lampoon's Lemmings* was to feature "The Woodshuck Festival of Love, Peace and Death," drawing a parallel to the sometimes mindless crowd logic at Woodstock, a three-day outdoor concert that turned into a cultural milestone of the 1960s. The concert-goers at Woodshuck were depicted as lemmings, pathetic creatures that simply followed whatever others were doing. The entertainment for the festival was to be made up of takeoffs of the entertainment that had been at the real Woodstock Festival.

Tony Hendra of *National Lampoon* was looking for someone who could do Joe Cocker. As soon as he caught Belushi's act, he knew he had to look no further. Not only did Hendra hire John to play Cocker, but John also wound up becoming the show's emcee.

John's move to New York naturally included Judy. Although the two were not married, they were still very much a couple. When Judy became homesick for Chicago, John was ready to pack it in and return to the Windy City. But the show's producers realized John's importance in the production and were not prepared to lose him. Because Judy was a talented artist, they were able to find work for her in *National Lampoon*'s art department. Immersed in their work, John and Judy decided to stick it out in New York.

The couple settled into a hectic but happy routine there. Their relationship was further cemented by the fact they had worked things out so they could both be productive. They would eventually marry on December 31, 1976. Once John's career took off and their financial situation improved, the two bought a summer home on Martha's Vineyard. But they would always keep a home in New York, and offices as well.

Lemmings opened in New York at the Gate Theater in January 1973, the day after John's 24th birthday. Even though Tony Hendra had made it quite clear that the cast was to be an ensemble in which everyone had equal billing, audiences and critics alike agreed: John was the star of the show. What's more, he was hailed in review after review as "funny."

For John, being the star of the show was important. He really wanted to make a name for himself. Being funny was important, too. More than anything, John wanted to make people laugh.

He later traveled as director of the *Lemmings* touring company, which included Chevy Chase and Bill Murray. Because of budget constraints, it was a short run. John stayed on with National Lampoon, however, working on both its *Radio Hour* and later with its briefly revived stage show in New York.

Writing and recruiting for Lampoon, John was on the lookout for potential performers. During a trip north to see Canada's Second City Comedy Troupe, he met Dan Aykroyd. Impressed by Aykroyd's talent, John offered Dan a job at National Lampoon in New York. Too busy to take on another assignment, Aykroyd promised Belushi he'd be in touch. Missing out on Aykroyd, John contented himself with having recruited Second City alumni Gilda Radner, Harold Ramis, and Joe Flaherty. Soon, John would follow Radner to a spot on a new late-night show.

Lorne Michaels had thought John Belushi was wrong for his new late-night television show, *Saturday Night*. Michaels had carefully crafted an ensemble cast including Gilda Radner, Chevy Chase, Garrett Morris, and Dan Aykroyd. He sought team players who would work together, and he was afraid that Belushi wanted the limelight for himself. But John's name kept coming up, and Michaels finally gave in and granted Belushi an audition.

Not many people show up for television auditions in an old bathrobe. But John did. When Michaels found himself laughing at John's insane samurai skit, he hired the pony-tailed, sword-swinging young man in the old bathrobe.

The samurai and other characters that Belushi created for *Saturday Night* would become legendary. Writing and performing with the other members of the "Not Ready for Prime Time Players" as their ensemble cast was known, John came into his own. He pleaded with Lorne Michaels to rely more on live performances from the talented cast and less on guests, musical acts, and pretaped segments. Slowly, as the show became increasingly popular and the Not Ready for Prime Time Players became stars in their own right, Michaels warmed to John's way of thinking. The show's new name, *Saturday Night Live,* which was adopted at the beginning of the third season, reflected the change.

The show had been evolving since it first began on October 11, 1975. John convinced Lorne Michaels to let him re-create his dead-on Joe Cocker impersonation for the third show that aired. He managed to nail Cocker's vocals, despite all the jerky gyrations. As always, John poured everything he had into the sketch.

Mimicking others' voices was a Belushi specialty. Playing Ludwig von Beethoven composing at the piano, John knitted his trademark arched eyebrows as he launched into a rendition of "My Girl" with a German accent. Later, his Beethoven would don a pair of dark sunglasses and rock back and forth doing his best Ray Charles as he sang "Baby, It's Allright." Gilda Radner and Laraine Newman were his hysterically funny, historically incorrect backup singers.

He played the Incredible Hulk to Bill Murray's Superman, and Captain James T. Kirk to Chevy Chase's Mr. Spock in a parody of *Star Trek*. He played Humphrey Bogart to Candice Bergen's Ingrid Bergman in a *Casablanca* sketch, and Jack Nicholson's McMurphy—in a bee costume, no less—to Raquel Welch's Nurse Ratched in "One Flew Over the Hornet's Nest," a spoof of *One Flew Over the Cuckoo's Nest*.

Most of John's *SNL* sketches were performed live, and allowances had to be made for studio audience reaction. When he was in costume portraying Marlon Brando's *Godfather*, he had to stay in character and pause whenever the audience roared with laughter. Wearing a black gown and a black wig, playing the part of glamorous but overweight movie star Elizabeth Taylor, John performed the Heimlich maneuver on himself as his Liz choked on some chicken. Interviewer Bill Murray managed to keep a straight face as he calmly continued his questions, despite the fact that John's Taylor was dramatically gasping for air.

Offscreen and onstage, Dan Aykroyd and John Belushi were the best of friends. John played Jackie Gleason's Ralph Kramden, while Dan played Art Carney's Norton. John took on the role of Henry Kissinger while Dan played President Nixon. John sang lead as Dan played harmonica while they, and the entire band behind them, wore black-and-yellow bee costumes.

Together, Belushi and Aykroyd launched their own pet project—the Blues Brothers—as musical guests appearing on *Saturday Night Live*.

John and cheerleaders in *Animal House*.

MAKING MOVIES

Over the course of his career, National Lampoon seemingly was always there for John. Besides *Lemmings* and its *Radio Hour*, in 1977 he was approached by fledgling film director John Landis, who wanted John as Bluto for National Lampoon's first movie, *Animal House*. Actually, there was a little more to it than that. Landis didn't just hope for John—he absolutely, positively, had to have John for the film.

At this point in his short career, John Landis didn't have a lot of leverage. He had just wrapped up his first film project. *Kentucky Fried Movie* hadn't cost much to make, but it had demonstrated to Universal Studios that Landis was capable of pulling off satire, a type of humor that pokes fun at something else. In his *Kentucky Fried Movie*, Landis had spoofed certain television shows and movies. In *Animal House*, Landis would be required to satirize anything and everything regarding life on a college campus during the early 1960s.

Universal wasn't about to hand such an ambitious project over to an inexperienced director without some sort of ace in the hole. They needed their first movie project with the nationally acclaimed satirists of National Lampoon to be a success—and they looked to John.

There was no question that John could pull off satire. He was currently poking fun at nearly every aspect of American life while appearing live from New York on television every Saturday night. But more important than that, John didn't have to prove anything to the folks at National Lampoon. They knew his work and loved it.

Regardless of the medium—radio, television, or live theater—John had audiences all over America laughing hysterically. There was little doubt that his popularity would carry over to the big screen. So for *Animal House*, John would be the critical puzzle piece to pull the whole project together. Universal Studios spelled things out clearly for John Landis: get John Belushi, or there will be no *Animal House*.

Landis got his man and his movie. John signed a contract for $35,000 to play a fraternity party animal named John "Bluto" Blutarsky. Released in July of 1978, *Animal House* broke existing box office records for top gross receipts for a comedy film. It made John's crossover into filmmaking a success.

Not one to turn down work, John accepted another offer as well, a small part in a Jack Nicholson film to be shot in Mexico. John had been promised that his part would be finished filming in time for him to report to work for the beginning of his third season of *Saturday Night Live,* so he wouldn't be jeopardizing his television career. He'd be gaining experience in the movie-making business before he had to film *Animal House.*

He'd mimicked Nicholson's *One Flew Over the Cuckoo's Nest* character in a *SNL* skit; now he'd be getting a chance to work with Nicholson himself. Plus, John explained to his manager, Bernie Brillstein, he had one more reason to take the part. "My father always wanted to see me on a horse."

Goin' South was a quirky comedy that was pure Nicholson, who was also the film's director. An observant John quickly realized that he was but a bit player in the movie. Nicholson had the leading role both on and off the screen. He had assembled the cast and crew, and he was in charge. Things were done the way Nicholson wanted them done.

Nicholson's talented hodgepodge of actors included a trio from television. From the television series *Taxi* came bug-eyed Christopher Lloyd playing a lawman, as well as Danny DeVito in the role of a good-natured outlaw. John himself was coming straight from *Saturday Night Live,* the hottest late-night show on television. To the mix, Nicholson added newcomer Mary Steenburgen as his strong-minded leading lady, Julia.

John's character, Hector, factors into the movie only briefly. During the film's opening, he is part of a melee that takes place on horseback in the Rio Grande as Nicholson's character is first captured. Later, Hector leads Henry's horse up the ramp to the gallows to auction off the animal. It is then that the audience becomes aware that the long-haired lawman with the huge hat and the Mexican accent is John Belushi.

John was playing a role that used to be standard fare in many old westerns—that of an overweight, dim-witted Mexican. His fans were understandably disappointed—John only had a bit part in the film.

Unfortunately, despite the fact that John's screen time was short, the movie ran long during its filming. John was forced to commute between *Goin' South*'s Mexican location in Durango and New York City for the first several episodes of the new *Saturday Night Live* season. It gave him no downtime whatsoever and left him exhausted.

But there was no time to rest—soon he'd be filming *Animal House*. Written by Harold Ramis, Douglas Kenney, and Chris Miller, it was set at fictitious Faber College in 1962. Ramis, Kenney, and Miller had lived through the time of social upheaval and change that was the 1960s and had witnessed that the idyllic days of the early '60s hadn't lasted.

John's Bluto and his collegiate brethren at Delta House wreaked all sorts of havoc on their unfortunate Faber College. The make-believe college came to life on the campus of the University of Oregon at Eugene. More than 50 other colleges had rejected Landis's requests for permission to film on their campuses. But, for 30 days, the University of Oregon was transformed into Faber College, with some very interesting members in its student body.

First and foremost was John as Bluto, a man who spoke few words and drank many beers. Tim Matheson's character, Eric Stratton, welcomed pledges Larry Kroger (played by Tom Hulce) and Kent Dorfman (Stephen Furst) to the

John (front row, center) with his fraternity brothers in *Animal House*.

less-than-traditional Delta House. And then there was a young, curly-haired Donald Sutherland playing English professor Dave Jennings, who shared with his students a dislike for the poet John Milton and a fondness for smoking marijuana.

Missing from the movie was Dan Aykroyd, who was offered the part of the mad motorcyclist, D-Day, but who chose instead to spend his time writing. The role that John had wanted his friend to fill was handled instead by Bruce McGill. McGill's D-Day makes the only entrance in the film that threatens to upstage those made by John. He bursts through the doors of Delta House riding a motorcycle, revving it up a staircase, then introducing himself by tapping out his unique rendition of the "William Tell Overture" on his neck.

It was an impressive, albeit young, cast, even without Aykroyd. However, there was no doubt that John was the drawing card. It was John who brought his fans into the theaters, anxious to see what he was up to on the big screen.

In the opening scene of the film, freshmen Kroger and Dorfman are made to feel less than welcome at Omega House, where the name badge girl quickly dismisses the two as "a wimp and a blimp." Eager to pledge a fraternity—any fraternity—they continue their quest to find one that will accept them.

Dorfman figures that he has an "in" at Delta House since his brother is a member, but Kroger isn't exactly sold on the Delta fraternity. Just as he confesses, "I hear Delta is the worst house on campus," comes the sound of glass breaking as the nude torso and legs of a mannequin fly through a window, eventually landing at their feet. The strains of "Louie, Louie" by the Kingsmen suddenly pour through the shattered window.

Gingerly stepping over the mannequin, Kroger and Dorfman come across an upperclassman wearing a letter jacket, his back turned to them. They inquire, "Is this Delta House?" When he turns to answer, it becomes clear that Delta's notorious sergeant at arms, Bluto, had been relieving himself on the bushes.

So it was that John made his first appearance on-screen in *Animal House*. A happy drunk, Bluto cheerfully waved the two freshmen in, sloshing beer from his huge brandy snifter on them as he stumbled back into the frat house, cordially offering the boys free beer.

Right from the start, John established his character as a good-natured party animal and set a humorous if somewhat destructive tone for the film. Each time his character subsequently appeared on the screen, audiences were prepared to laugh. Director Landis focused on John's eyebrows and facial expressions for maximum comic effect, even reportedly cutting dialogue from the script in order to give John's expressive face its due.

John didn't have to say a word as he crushed a beer can on his forehead for emphasis. Nor did he need dialogue as he emerged from beneath the bleachers after watching two cheerleaders seated there ready themselves for practice. His grin and his eyebrows expressed his true sentiments.

He also didn't have to say a word when he checked his watch during the climactic parade scene; his impish grin said it all. Every other member of Delta House had checked their synchronized watches, most of which read precisely 11 o'clock. Bluto's read an incongruous 5:37, but he smiled knowingly, just the same, somehow aware that it was time for their planned mission to be carried out.

But not all of John's laughs relied on silent gestures. His response to the fraternity being put on "Double Secret Probation" was a frenzied chant, "Toga! Toga! Toga!" The infamous toga party scene that followed has since inspired countless college kids to don sheets as party attire. During the "Shout!" dance number, John's dance partner was his real-life wife, Judy. Besides her cameo appearance, she also worked on the film as a production associate.

John's character Bluto also gave the world the immortal words *"Food fight!"* in the midst of a comic chase scene through the campus cafeteria. No doubt administrators nationwide still regret that infamous call to action whenever they are called upon to calm down a frenzied school lunchroom.

When things got really bad and the college closed down Delta House, the academically impaired Bluto lamented, "Seven years of college down the drain!" His despair became deeper when he realized that not only was Delta no longer an accepted fraternity, it also wasn't a drinking establishment. "They took the bar!" he cried.

Even after the pot-smoking professor got a group of students stoned, Delta's Boon (Peter Riegart) did nothing more mischievous than croon a silly duet of "Hey, Paula," with his equally giddy sweetheart, Katy. Audiences learned that the debutante seen driving off with Bluto Blutarsky in a convertible stolen from the homecoming parade later became the wife of *Senator* Blutarsky.

That *Animal House* is a funny movie is largely owing to the outrageous on-screen persona of John Belushi. The film has been imitated many times, but no imitation comes close to being as funny as the original.

After *Animal House* there could be no turning back. The public clamored for more from John. The comedian did his best to accommodate his fans by cranking out two more movies.

In *1941* John was Wild Bill Kelso, piloting a plane over Los Angeles, trying to defend America against Japanese air attacks. His larger-than-life Kelso was a loner who interacted little with the rest of the film's massive cast. His scenes were truly fly-bys, interspersed throughout the movie as part of a rambling plot. John's high-flying Kelso was literally above the petty dance hall brawling and chaotic attempts at peacekeeping, strategically misdirected on the ground by Dan Aykroyd's character.

Aykroyd, Treat Williams, Tim Matheson, and John Candy were all immersed in scenes involving scores of military men and women, as well as civilians. Except for refueling stops and a crash landing here and there, Kelso had only his plane for company.

The Steven Spielberg film flopped, but it wasn't John's doing. He had turned in an amusing performance as a cigar-chomping, extra-macho wartime pilot with a case of paranoia.

As his popularity grew, fans wanted more of John on the big screen. Expectations on the part of the public can cause problems for performers. Moviegoers were eager to see John

John in *1941*.

in *Old Boyfriends*. But they were expecting to see him in a starring role opposite actress Talia Shire of *Rocky* fame. Since John was best known for his comedy, they were expecting John's role to be funny. They wanted Bluto, Part II.

John's character was only one of three old boyfriends, and as such, only on-screen during a third of the movie. The part entailed only six days' worth of filming. The versatile Belushi embraced the small but dramatic role wholeheartedly, especially since it called for him to sing as a member of a small-time rock and roll band.

His fine performance impressed his director, Joan Tewkesbury, and leading lady Shire. But John's public felt ripped off. They hadn't expected to see John Belushi's character get his comeuppance from a girl he had humiliated in high school.

John's character, Katz, had led his friends to believe that the two had had sex, when in truth, they had not. Sixteen years later, Shire's character would have the last laugh. Promising a romantic encounter she has no intention of having, she entices Katz, then drives off, leaving John's character standing defenseless in his socks, shoes, and shirt, having taken his pants and his pride.

Dan Aykroyd and John Belushi were siblings Elwood and Jake Blues in *The Blues Brothers*.

BROTHERS BLUE

John Belushi and Dan Aykroyd were accustomed to having to come up with their own comedy material. Both had begun creating characters and skits as members of the Second City Comedy Troupes, with John performing in Chicago and Dan in Toronto. When their careers came together during the years of *Saturday Night Live,* they were responsible for writing skits on a weekly basis along with the other *SNL* cast members.

Just as some of the material the two had created during their Second City days later turned up in *SNL* skits, so too did an *SNL* routine spill over into a full-fledged movie. Aykroyd and Belushi had honed their nightclub act in their private blues bar even before bringing it to television.

John and Dan transformed into their alter egos, Jake and Elwood Blues, respectively. Garbed in black suits with white shirts and skinny ties, Jake and Elwood appeared onstage wearing dark hats and sunglasses. Jake had to unlock the handcuffs linking Elwood's wrist to his briefcase so that Elwood could extract his blues harp with a flourish and begin to wail away on the harmonica. Both Blues Brothers then danced with fitful bursts of energy as Jake belted out his rendition of "Hey, Bartender."

Once the act was well received on television, it was only a matter of time before Jake and Elwood would take on the silver screen and the concert world. Although the characters of Jake and Elwood were funny, John and Dan were serious about the music. They put together a legitimate band, and Aykroyd, who had never before written a movie, came up with a huge, unwieldy script. *The Blues Brothers* wound up becoming a magnet for blues musicians wanting to be a part of the project, both on the screen and on the concert tour.

John Landis helped Aykroyd polish the script and signed on as the film's director. He even had a cameo in the movie as Trooper LaForge.

The film opens at the Joliet Correction Center in Illinois, as a man clad in prison blues is escorted by two armed guards through the prison yard to the clerk's office. He has been granted parole for good behavior. As the prisoner drums his fingers on the countertop, awaiting the return of his worldly possessions, the tattoos on his fingers spell out his identity: J-A-K-E.

Just as Joliet Jake Blues is being handed his belongings, including his signature sunglasses and hat, a driver en route to the prison is seen tightly gripping the steering wheel of a reclaimed police cruiser, revealing a set of similarly tattooed knuckles: E-L-W-O-O-D. Thus is the audience introduced to the Blues Brothers.

Jake and Elwood were raised in the St. Helen of the Blessed Shroud Orphanage. Dutiful brother that he is, Elwood picks up Jake from prison and proceeds directly to the orphanage, having promised Sister Mary Stigmata that he would bring Jake by as soon as he's sprung from the slammer. The brothers soon learn that the orphanage is in trouble and will be forced to close its doors unless taxes totaling $5,000 are paid. Jake and Elwood don't need to hear more. Their mission is clear. They must raise the money for the woman they call the Penguin, the formidable nun who raised them in the only home they've ever known.

Everything comes to Jake in a flash of light during a rousing sermon given by the godfather of soul, James Brown, who plays the Reverend Cleophus James. Jake has it all figured out. They'll get the band back together, play a few gigs, and turn the money over to the taxman for the Penguin.

As if rounding up all the members of the band weren't going to be difficult enough, Elwood is pulled over for failing to stop at a red light. When the police learn that he's driving with a revoked driver's license, Elwood decides to take his

The Blues Brothers.

chances trying to outrun the cops in the movie's first high-speed chase. *The Blues Brothers* would become known for its hilarious car chases. Never before in film history had so many police cruisers become so entangled and rendered so helpless.

The two go about rounding up the band, encountering Aretha Franklin and Ray Charles along the way. Wearing the pink uniform of her Soul Food Cafe, Franklin belts out a soulful rendition of "Think" as she tries to discourage her character's husband, Matt "Guitar" Murphy, from rejoining the Blues Brothers Band. Ray Charles, playing a music store owner, inspires an impromptu block party when he launches into "Shake a Tail Feather" to prove that a keyboard still works.

Still dodging the police and miraculously surviving the repeated attempts of Jake's old girlfriend to kill them both, Jake and Elwood manage to get the band back together. Jake's first attempt at finding them work proves disastrous when they take to the stage at Bob's Country Bunker. Accustomed to country and western music, the crowd starts pelting the band with beer bottles.

Thinking on his feet, Elwood huddles the band together, and they hastily switch gears, launching into the western-flavored theme from TV's *Rawhide*. Jake finds a bullwhip nearby and cracks it soundly to enhance the song. This satisfies the Bunker's rowdy crowd and has the film's audiences laughing at the odd juxtaposition of a blues band playing such a song.

Eventually the band does get to play a bona fide concert to a packed house. The legendary Cab Calloway, as Curtis, has helped in recruiting orphans to promote the concert and even opens the show himself when Jake and Elwood are further delayed after the bluesmobile runs out of gas.

When Jake and Elwood do finally take the stage, it takes a while for the crowd to warm to their act. But once they do, the frenzied, rhythmic clapping makes it possible for Jake and Elwood to slip off the darkened stage unnoticed while the band continues to play.

Backstage, they are met by a record producer who wants to record them and who fronts them enough money to pay the taxes for the orphanage. He also allows them to give each band member his fair share, plus money to settle other debts.

Unfortunately, because a large part of the concert audience is out to get Jake and Elwood, including everyone from the country and western band whose gig they stole, to the police, to Jake's demented girlfriend, the brothers don't stick around for an encore. Exiting through an onstage trapdoor, they begin their hazardous journey to the tax collector's office.

Their trip is an eventful one, since the local law enforcement agencies have mounted a massive offensive to capture Jake and Elwood. But the brothers persevere, managing to hand over the money to none other than the film's producer, Steven Spielberg, playing a cameo role as the tax collector.

John "Jake Blues" Belushi.

Dan Akyroyd and John Belushi came to realize that they could not sustain the frenetic pace of the film in their own lives any longer. Making movies, touring as a blues band, and appearing in a weekly live television show left them little time to relax. Something had to give. Reluctantly, Dan and John announced that they would not be returning to *Saturday Night Live* for the next season.

The Belushi and Aykroyd years at *SNL*, from the show's inception in 1975 until their departure in 1979, are still considered by many to be among the show's best.

John with Blair Brown in *Continental Divide.*

DIVIDING A CONTINENT

In the romantic comedy *Continental Divide,* John Belushi's character, Ernie Souchak, finds himself embroiled in the classic struggles of modern literature—man against man, man against himself, and man against nature. Through it all, Souchak perseveres, climbs to the mountain's top, overcomes his addiction to cigarettes, and wins the girl, all while managing to continue his muckraking in his column for a Chicago newspaper.

Although it would be disappointing to some fans expecting John's typical lunacy, the film would nonetheless be accepted by those who enjoy romantic comedies. It would also be heartily endorsed by the man upon whom John's character was loosely based, Mike Royko.

When the movie was released, Royko's column for the day reflected the good-natured ribbing Royko had received from his friends about having been portrayed on-screen by John Belushi. After all, John was best known for his outlandish comedy and did not exactly fit the mold of the typical handsome leading man. But that did not faze Royko. He was proud to have one of the Belushi boys playing a Royko-based newspaperman on the screen.

John's Ernie Souchak is a confirmed bachelor, content with his column and his celebrity status in Chicago. Hot on the scent of a corrupt politician named Yablonowitz, Souchak's columns come dangerously close to the scandalous unfolding drama. To keep his star columnist out of harm's way, Souchak's editor suggests that Souchak lay low for a while and convinces him to go on assignment and get the lowdown on an eagle expert high in the Rockies.

John's city boy out of his element was both funny and endearing, as he trekked behind the hired guide leading him to

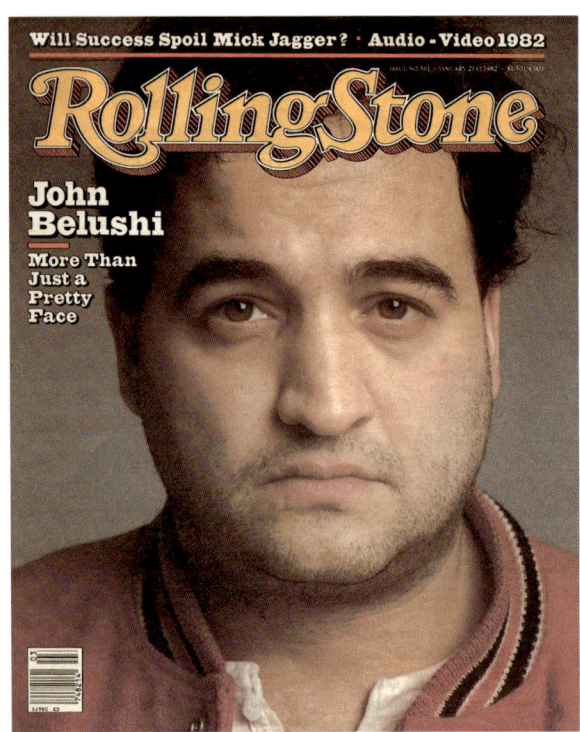

John on the cover of *Rolling Stone*, January 1982.

Nell Porter's remote cabin. Gasping for breath in the thin mountain air, Souchak passes out after a single puff on what was about to become one of his last cigarettes. Moments later, curious bears ransack his backpack and take most of his smokes.

At first, Nell Porter, played by Blair Brown, is none too happy about having an uninvited reporter drop in to do a story about her. But as time wears on she begins to view Ernie as less of an opponent, and in turn, her resourcefulness comes to impress him. When he takes a nasty tumble down a snow-covered slope, she single-handedly manufactures a stretcher of sorts and drags him all the way back to the cabin.

Just when his injured back is nearly mended, he is attacked by a mountain lion. As she nurses him through this latest setback, Nell and Ernie realize they've fallen in love, just before he must return to Chicago.

A lovesick and disheveled Souchak mopes around the newspaper offices, unable to write until a back-page news item stirs him back to social consciousness. Souchak's former source has been found dead. Knowing his friend's fear of heights, he immediately suspects foul play on the part of Yablonowitz. Suddenly, Souchak swings back into action, filling his columns with accusations so accurate that his own apartment is blown up in retaliation.

When Nell visits Chicago with her campaign to save the eagles, Ernie almost doesn't attend her lecture, but he can't stay away. And once he hears her voice and sees her face, he realizes how he still feels about her. They spend the rest of her visit together, with Ernie playing host, showing her Chicago as she had shown him the eagles and the wilderness.

Because both of their careers are so cemented in their unique locations, they reluctantly admit that geography must keep them apart. In the end, however, Ernie's failed attempts at saying good-bye at the train station have him winding up in Wyoming. Nell and Ernie are married quickly by a justice of the peace before he boards the next train back to Chicago, with promises to see each other when the snow melts.

John in probably his best-known film, *Animal House*.

After filming on location high in the mountains of Colorado, the cast and crew of *Continental Divide* moved on to shoot the city scenes of Chicago, where John was much more in his element. Finally, the interior scenes were finished up in Los Angeles.

But just as Souchak had been able to give up cigarettes while roughing it in the Rockies and succumbed again to the habit, so did John abandon many of his healthy habits once the crew hit his hometown. By the time the production landed in L.A., Belushi was struggling to stay drug-free.

Dan Aykroyd, John Belushi, and Cathy Moriarty in *Neighbors.*

FAREWELL TO A FRIEND

John felt a general sense of happiness and self-pride at the start of filming for *Continental Divide*. By the time he and Dan Aykroyd became totally immersed in their next project, *Neighbors*, that feeling was gone. The dark comedy was proving difficult to bring to the screen.

John had come to understand what it was that his fans expected to see. He realized they had been disappointed by his small roles in both *Goin' South* and *Old Boyfriends*. He knew that even his starring role as Ernie Souchak wouldn't satisfy the fans who were accustomed to his usual zany comedy. As a result, he had misgivings about some of the proposed ideas for *Neighbors*.

Normally, Aykroyd played the straight man, while John tended to play the more outrageous characters. Their roles were reversed in *Neighbors*. Dan dyed his hair blond and wore crazy getups throughout the entire film, at one point donning a wet suit, compete with snorkel and mask, while John wore a three-piece suit. Aykroyd's Vic was a nightmare of a neighbor, while John's Earl Keese was a contented family man.

As production on *Neighbors* wore on, John became more and more aware that the movie wasn't working. He wanted to have the director, John Avildsen, fired and replaced with someone who was more comfortable doing comedy.

With all the good stuff Belushi and Aykroyd had offered on camera, Avildsen hadn't successfully spliced together a funny movie. Belushi and Aykroyd did their best to make the most of the movie, but there was little they could do to salvage a comedy that just wasn't humorous.

John wanted desperately to compensate for the failure of *Neighbors* by making his next movie project, *Sweet Deception*, a huge success. He sought out Don Novello, who had portrayed Father Guido Sarducci on *Saturday Night Live*. It was Novello who had taken the stories John had shared with him about his father and uncle in their diner days and had written the hilarious sketch that everyone remembered for its constant chant of "Cheezbugga, cheezbugga."

Because the film was to be about the wine country, John went on a tour of vineyards. He worked hard on its details, and to a degree, its script, round the clock, for weeks on end. Because Novello lived in California, John bunkered down in a bungalow he rented at the Chateau Marmont so that he could be in close contact with his screenwriting partner. Novello was left to do most of the writing, as John was becoming increasingly concerned with minute details regarding the movie, and less and less coherent due to a lack of sleep and an increasing reliance on drugs.

John had learned how to ward off sleep by snorting cocaine while working long hours. Usually, he would swear off cocaine for a time after completing a project, but unfortunately, cocaine was all too accessible, and John found it nearly impossible to resist. It was popular at parties and could be found easily on the street or in a bar.

The script for *Sweet Deception,* which John had retitled *Noble Rot,* had taken far too long to write, and once it was finally finished, it was poorly received by everyone in Hollywood who read it. John's usually solid comedic judgment had been impaired too much for far too long by too much coke and too little sleep. The film was never made.

Dan Aykroyd tried to convince his friend to put the script aside for a while. Dan explained to John that rewrites were a part of the business and not to be overly concerned.

Judy wanted John home, too. She knew that L.A., its drugs, and John alone were a recipe for disaster. She talked with Dan. They were both apprehensive about each additional day John spent out in California alone.

Finally, John called Dan to tell him he would be taking the red-eye flight home to New York. But he later called Judy to say that there was one more meeting he had to attend, and that he'd have to spend another day on the West Coast.

It was one day too many. John Belushi died on March 5, 1982. His trainer, Bill Wallace, found John's lifeless body when he stopped by the bungalow about noon to drop off a typewriter. Wallace tried desperately to revive his friend, but he was too late. By the coroner's office's estimate, John died almost two hours before Wallace arrived.

John wasn't a heroin addict. In 1977, after damaging cartilage in his knee as he leapt awkwardly from a stage, he had looked elsewhere for relief when his prescription drugs had failed to alleviate the pain. He had tried heroin. He quickly realized how dangerous heroin was and had sworn off the stuff.

And yet, heroin, mixed with cocaine, injected into his veins by one Catherine Evelyn Smith, was what killed John Belushi. Tired and strung out, John had gone out seeking some coke. He found Smith, a heroin addict with access to any number of drugs, who could do what John could never bring himself to do—inject himself with a needle. Smith had injected John and herself with a combination of heroin and cocaine, called a speedball, several times during the night and the early hours of the morning. Accustomed to the highs and lows associated with heroin use, Smith took the hits in stride. John didn't. The sleep that John had been avoiding for days finally came. He never woke up.

Instead of getting down to work with John on one of their pending projects, Dan Aykroyd found himself with the task of telling Judy that John was dead. Together, Dan and Judy got through that evening as family and friends began to gather at John and Judy's home. They buried their beloved John on Martha's Vineyard as snow fell.

At the time of John's death, a plethora of projects that were to have involved him were on the drawing boards of many of Hollywood's writers, directors, and producers. And more than a few friends and colleagues felt as if they could have done more to prevent John's premature death.

Director Louis Malle regretted that his planned *Moon Over*

Miami project hadn't been ready to absorb John's energies and talent. John Landis, Steven Spielberg, Lorne Michaels, Robin Williams, and others all wished they had been able to make a difference and somehow prevent John's death.

And yet, those who knew him best, including his beloved Judy and his best friend, Dan Aykroyd, realized that there was only so much that anyone could have done, for John's was an addictive personality.

None other than "Uncle Mike" Royko came to John's posthumous defense, when his readers blasted him for his relationship with a drug addict. Royko wrote in his syndicated column on March 16, 1982, "Belushi hurt no one but himself, and his family."

Judy Jacklin Belushi compiled a loving televised tribute to her late husband that she called "West Heaven." Devastated by John's death, she kept journals, which she crafted into the book *Samurai Widow*. She later remarried.

John's buddy Bill Murray stepped in to become the Ghostbuster that John was to have been. Belushi's brother Jim joined the cast of *SNL* for a time and became a Blues Brother as well. But Jim Belushi was not replacing his big brother in either capacity. An actor in his own right, Jim has put together an impressive body of work onstage and in film.

Dan Aykroyd has continued his film career. With an 18-year hiatus between the original and the sequel, he brought the blues back to the silver screen with *Blues Brothers 2000*.

Aykroyd stood alongside John's brother Jim during *Saturday Night Live*'s 15th anniversary special to introduce clips featuring John's work on the show. When the amalgamated cast of *Saturday Night Live* assembled on the occasion of the show's 25th anniversary, Dan Aykroyd and Laraine Newman shared the duties of introducing some of John Belushi's best sketches.

At the show's end, posing for a group photograph, Dan sat solo, front and center, alone in the first row. There was no mistaking who should have been sitting beside him.

Further Reading

Belushi, Judith Jacklin. *Samurai Widow*. New York: Carroll & Graf Publishers, 1990.

Royko, Mike. *One More Time: The Best of Mike Royko*. Chicago: University of Chicago Press, 1999.

Woodward, Bob. *Wired: The Short Life and Fast Times of John Belushi*. New York: Simon & Schuster, 1984.

Chronology

1949   Adam and Agnes Belushi welcome son John on January 24.
1967   John graduates from Wheaton Central High School in Illinois; attends the University of Wisconsin at Whitewater.
1968   Drops out of U of W and enrolls in the College of DuPage.
1970   Graduates on January 5 with an associates of the arts degree in general studies.
1971   At age 22, John Belushi becomes the youngest-ever member of Chicago's Second City Comedy Troupe.
1972   *National Lampoon* hires Belushi. He tours with *Lemmings*.
1973   Meets Dan Aykroyd for the first time, in Canada.
1975   *Saturday Night* begins its run on NBC.
1976   Marries Judith Jacklin on New Year's Eve in Colorado.
1978   Aykroyd and Belushi make their network television debut as the Blues Brothers on *SNL*; *Animal House* and *Goin' South* are released.
1979   *Old Boyfriends* and *1941* are released; John leaves the cast of *SNL*; the Blues Brothers' first album is number one on the charts.
1980   *The Blues Brothers* is released.
1981   *Continental Divide* is released; Belushi and Aykroyd are paired again on the big screen in *Neighbors*.
1982   John Belushi dies of a drug overdose in California on March 5.

Filmography

Television
1975–79   *Saturday Night Live*
1977   *Things We Did Last Summer*
1978   *The Rutles* (spoof of the Beatles)

Movies
1978   *Goin' South*
         Animal House
1979   *Old Boyfriends*
         1941
1980   *The Blues Brothers*
1981   *Continental Divide*
         Neighbors

INDEX

Animal House (movie), 5, 6, 14, 23–24, 25–29
Aykroyd, Dan, 19–20, 21, 26, 27, 29, 33, 34, 37, 43, 44, 45, 46
Belushi, Adam (father), 9, 11–12, 14
Belushi, Agnes (mother), 9
Belushi, Billy (brother), 9
Belushi, Jim (brother), 9, 46
Belushi, John
 birth of, 9
 childhood of, 9–10
 death of, 45–46
 and drug abuse, 6–7, 13, 18, 41, 44–46
 education of, 10, 11, 12, 13–15
 family of, 9–10
 and interest in acting, 11–12, 15
 wedding of, 19
Belushi, Judy Jacklin (wife), 6, 7, 10–11, 12, 13, 14, 15, 18–19, 28, 44, 45, 46
Belushi, Marian (sister), 9
Beshekas, Steve, 15
Blues Brothers, 7, 21, 33–36, 46
Blues Brothers, (TV sketch), 33
Blues Brothers, The (movie), 6, 33–36
Blues Brothers 2000 (movie), 46
Brillstein, Bernie, 24
Chase, Chevy, 19, 20, 21
Cocker, Joe, 17, 18, 20
College of DuPage, 15
Continental Divide (movie), 5–7, 39–41, 43
Goin' South (movie), 24–25, 43
Hendra, Tony, 18, 19
Insana, Tino, 15
John Loves Mary (summer theater), 13
Landis, John, 23, 28, 34, 46
Malle, Louis, 45

Michaels, Lorne, 20, 46
Moon Over Miami (proposed film), 45–46
Murray, Bill, 19, 21, 46
National Lampoon, 18–20, 23
Neighbors (movie), 43
Newman, Laraine, 21, 46
Nicholson, Jack, 21, 24–25
1941 (movie), 5, 6, 29
Novello, Don, 43–44
Old Boyfriends (movie), 31, 43
Payne, Dan, 11–12, 13, 15
Radner, Gilda, 20, 21
Rehner, Adrian, 11–12
Royko, Mike, 5, 6, 39, 46
Sahlins, Bernard, 17
Samurai Widow, (Judy Belushi), 10, 46
Saturday Night Live (TV), 6, 9, 20–21, 24, 25, 33, 37, 46
Second City Comedy Troupe, 6, 13, 17–18, 19–20, 33
Shawnee Summer Theater, 11–13, 15, 17, 18
Shire, Talia, 31
Smith, Catherine Evelyn, 45
Spielberg, Steven, 5, 6, 7, 29, 36, 46
Sweet Deception (proposed film), 43–44
Tender Trap, The (summer theater), 13
University of Wisconsin at Whitewater, 12, 13–15
Wallace, Bill, 7, 45
Wendell, Smokey, 7
West Compass Players, 15
Wheaton Central High School, 10, 11, 14
Wired: The Short Life and Fast Times of John Belushi (Woodward), 5